A Sea of Other

A Sea of Other

Poems by

Steven Joyce

Cover design by Shay Culligan

ISBN: 978-1-949229-24-0

Kelsay Books
Aldrich Press
www.kelsaybooks.com

For my wife, wanderers, and other children of alterity . . .

"… to be really human [. . .] is probably to be unavoidably sentimental and naïve and goo-prone and generally pathetic."
David Foster Wallace, *Infinite Jest*

"When you're strange / Faces come out of the rain / When you're strange / No one remembers your name /when you're strange."
Jim Morrison

Acknowledgements

The following poems appeared in www. *Poetry Magazine*.com, "Editor's Choice," summer 2014.

When Birnam Wood Walks on Two Feet

New Year's Recall (Redux)

On the Job

She 1

The Wrong Fold: Evolution's Next Story

Snow on the Roof

I am especially grateful to Dr. Patrick Madigan, SJ, Dr. Norman Jones, and Eva Borkowska for their generosity of time as well as their continued support and encouragement in bringing this project to fruition.

Contents

A Sea of Other

I

On a sea of other
they huddle and undulate
coming ashore sick but happy, daubs of orange
falling out of flimsy boats that tip and capsize,
as roving bands of TV guys
pace the beach, sniff the air
for photogenic tragedy
and the smell of the day-old dead—
the soft flesh of promise
drowning in mere inches of broken water—
dying, no other word for it.

II

Sorry the TV guys say,
unable to resist the story line,
they fuss with their nesting dolls,
tucking small evils into larger evils—
nothing more compelling
than pathos that hides
fear inside of fear
death inside of death
like a babushka doll
scarved and plump
they smooth their hair,
rehearse their lines:
These faces have paid too much
for too little crossing these seas
that just as readily swallow them as buoy them.

III

The soft give of white sand
imprinting the weight of hope
makes them reckless with joy they dream
of homely routine and well-nourished prayers
of smoking a shisha
as they fall and flounder and drown.
Then life vests wash up, first one then more
the shore strewn with bodies sticking in the sand.
A photographer walks by and snaps
a photo that captures the ebb and flow and holds for ransom
a small death that sends the Furies scrambling
to bring someone to justice,
to undo the pixilated face and body.
Some kiss the ground, others each other in disbelief.
Some weep for this unknown Ithaca,
others wander the shore looking
for the way home, seeking something to salvage.

On the Job

They disappeared
on the job
in the job
faded into a habit of weak presence,
pulled into what seemed like non-issuance,
the gravity of swarm and sameness
keeping them low
they drank their mutualist drink
but gained little
from that tangled nectar
and milled about the hive
as if clearing offal,
the clarion buzz of institutional logic waking each
to wordy logarithms of thought:
"We are family if but for the hive
we are one, glad to be alive."

They seldom looked forward.
But when the transparency blurred
and pollen wrote messages like Ouija on the wall,
they looked for the prophet with double a hundred eyes
to tell them what they already knew.

They heard many times over
through honey and wax,
through bee stench and queen pride,
the precise sameness
the fatuous intensity
and were wowed by the invention
the apiary dreamt up.
"Just once," they thought, "to eat one's fill of honey
to wander from the bee line

to never fly straight
home to hive and heaven
to the small room with eight walls
where hotly contested they argued and ate their sandwiches
and with drooping proboscises watched
waited for the pollen to levitate.
It is then that some said, "We can't really fly, you know."
and they fell in a puff of pollen like quibbling angels
from and through the ether
that did not cushion the fall.

One day as usual,
they were not there.
they were not they.

They breathed the air of elsewhere
and ate their sandwiches, tuna scars and all
and with honeyed whiskered sounds
debated in big words if there was a god
just for bees.

She 1

The familiar one becomes silent,
smiles and fusses to smooth
her plaid housedress
stuffed with crumpled receipts,
memories bought and paid for,
some still in their original packing.

She sits in a dream, on a chair
that is brown and worn and cracked
where she rests her arms,
near the window that juts out onto the driveway
in the light that scatters dust motes she thinks
she's a child blowing
dandelion seeds to the wind.

The rude sun slings light at her
thick and yellow and miscreant.
She breathes, nonetheless
the fog that drifts in rings above her head,
cold rubble condemned to orbit
a past that recedes she disappears
hands in her lap
in upright inaccessibility
her smoker's rings dissolve upward,
her dreams cannot escape
the gravity of her silence.

The Paladin Sun

Orange and dirty a craven sun illuminates
flecks of panini and zoster virus on his lapel
orbiting like ions both attracting and repulsing.
He cannot spoon a single word face idea event
in this porridge of loss—
thick and lumpy lumps, smushed recall stunned,
sunk in a steam of stutter and stammer.

He cannot catch the errant breath,
that will not name the crime, he stares
into the pot of porridge
melts away and frightens us
as if a vortex, he might pull us in
this monster dissolution
this raw emptying so wicked
both angel in heaven and demon in hell
look away.

We look at each other with gimpy comprehension
and say the small question words in silence—
the few words of a prayer forgotten
that end up pointing to a broken God.
His eyes cloud and arch—some kind of nebula
comes into view,
throws dust into the darkness
blind gas to violent light,
a synapse flashes then flames out.

An orphan at breakfast his one thought
fidgets, forgets his parents
hates them for giving him life
for making this death so slow.

Against that smoky ambient sun
motes spin and float
between the cracks of planking
where the light is fierce
where skin furrows weightlessly—

the place where he lives.

The day has come
the time has come.
We bend our knees to pray
and raise our eyes as they do in films
and tug after him with baby whispers
that seat him
that feed him
and say *you remember when . . .?*

He says *yes,*
we curse him for mocking modest hope.
He smells the sughi on the stove
that will stain his shirt, trips him up the stairs
with a food memory that catches his feet, he falls,
forgets, calls for help
as a blotch of indelible time creeps
across his face—a moving birthmark—
we cringe they sigh
he smiles beneath eyes that watch
the eclipse of the paladin sun.

Sisyphus

To succeed in sledding
one needs the cold and forbidding
one needs to be
reckless mostly
in the choice of hills
and expository rationales
one needs blades that cut
the white stuff
that tracks the weight of being
deep and parallel to the slope and steep of it all.

Just enough Sisyphean steep
to freeze existential
drool and snot into philosophy,
this asynchronous speed down and away
to the edge of the ravine
to the senseless waters
that churn under the ice,
late winter and early spring mud
that softens the soils of contemplation as snow
softens to slush.

In places porous to thought,
one slows
and often sinks
and suffers.

To succeed in sledding, one needs
the slime-green stone the excitement around it
the glide and swoosh and pitch and eddy
of children holding hands
as the colding stone cheek
softens and blushes
with hope.

Snow on the Roof (Epilepsis)

it clings and tides, a hybrid storm
spread by howls and snarls
in sheaths of allknowing scatter—
a spoiled child on the brink of tantrum, a brain
once bright and bossy, the sun backs away
the froth and flailing curlscold neural sunlight
wind-rowed in high banks of stutter and stammer.

The chemical storm stops, worn
we watch from windows deep set
cataracted in milky grief and bleary awe.
The lattice work snaps back in place, each flake
they say the hand of god retired and painting
he admires his handiwork and decides he needs
some praise . . .

Our eyes blink and offer a prayer
that runs down one cheek scavenging
hope in clear cold space
as a local galaxy races away.

New Year's Recall (Redux)

Except for the New Year's
obituaries
famous people
and their last assigned words
gone
and the radio preacher
preaching dire certainties
swearing
"You would not expect that from a god
who dormed at the Temple Mount
and willed his beard white
to persuade us of His wisdom."

Except for that I might believe
that Providence works like investment theory
giving back paying interest compounding returns,
the divinity student hangs his hat on this
hoping it will pay off
hangs around Christ like a high school *cumbar*,
theological hormones running wild he wonders
if the investment is wise—
"Hanging on the tree," he reflects,
waiting for death and resurrection
with some trepidation I'm sure
the world will end
as others have said.
He knows and fills
the back row first,
acned, bored he nods,
the lacquer of proud ignorance and lame obeisance
suffocating and tainting the stars
he knows will vanish.

And we will punish ourselves for that,
he thinks,
with faith and hope
but leave true Sadness
for the Hollywood stars dead and dying,
anointing them in a ritual of
celluloid extreme unction,
an indulgence that frees them
in this purgatory of sameness.

This year of notable deaths,
has taught me this:
Repent the small sins first
and leverage the big ones later.

Thinking my soul is too big to fail
that god will bail
me out of this human mess
and compensate me for my Christian self-concern,
I think and speak and tie the Windsor knot
tight at the neck, a freshly pressed shirt
will speak for me.

This year's end the word *lachrymose* lets fall
a tear that distracts me with sadness,
Kitty Welles and Nora Ephron
nowhere
to be found.

If the Truth be Told

If the Truth be told,
it is habit—the protozoan kind—
an animal
small, unthinking, unlikely
to evolve quickly,
yet holds some promise
over Time.

It is gravity that pulls us upward
and covers us with the grated filings
of the last machine Age.

If the truth be told,
we shill to dapper vaudevillians—
politicians ridiculous but not funny,
who broker our ordinary gravitas
and leverage our loneliness.

We are latch-key children
who let ourselves in and snack
alone on religion and entitlement.

The seasons of truth—
springs and winters cagey and tideless,
summers and autumns witless and wane—
stare like the Arnolfinis—freakish and fecund
amid the clutter of prosperity and bad taste.

If the Truth be told,
we look to the comedians and priests and rock'n rollers
with equal hope of deliverance and wait
in deepest dryness
for conditions to moisten when we come to life
and emerge to a moonless self.

The Lame Satyr

The morning's lame
Satyr darts from rock to tree
pulls at his chambray comfortsizers his love elastic
a maenad-breath away
cloven-eyed he sees double
cloven-eared he hears troubling voices:

Did you sleep well and dream love?
Sit by me and sip your coffee I'll whisper
what I think into your fuzzy bifurcated ear,
dear stop twitching
I mean no harm . . .

not the first Siren to say that
to him hiding
from her pebbly gaze,
funky goat gunk in his eyes that well up
with uncomplicated tears,
irritation mostly, failing senses, some kind of onion
cut from maenad glint and mock sadness.

The morning adolescent sweet and tingling dumb
he hears a treacly giggle
he smells orchid perfume
he descends Duchamp-like
that elusive staircase sliding his goat-hands along
the mahogany banister.

The infirm *tragos* hears
laughter from the trees and the sound of dirge
from the forest a little hoarse with grief
he concludes that all is well,
that lame goat-love while cloven
remains sure-footed.

The Wrong Fold: Evolution's Next Story

The perforation waiting
to tear
lay below that faux fold—
that unmeant crease
on the face of this billed life
as if
that was where it would happen
where it would grate and grind and slip
then shudder and gag up a small tsunami
racing unseen in watery clarity
until it reaches the outcroppings of misgiving
where it wells and smashes,
a rearing wall of muddy words
making garbage of everything
washing it away, stupefied.

It happens but not here
not at that design juncture
where what we owe,
tears away from what we are.

It happens where
your feet touch the floor where
your head indents the pillow where
crumbs drop from the table.

It drains only to return
to swallow that smudge of humanity on the beach
recumbent and bracing

giggling at the expenditure of impersonal vengeance
to bring one to heel
to toss one like a fur seal
in the mouth of an Orca.

The sheer ridiculous destruction,
nature's wastrel laughing last:
"I did not expect this" the tune
driven from the mouth
exiled into a very short prayer
that begins:
"No, not like this"
 and ends—"Please, not in this."

Izzy and Michael Bublé

I have begun
to listen
to Michael Bublé
and have come
to believe
I am
what he says
I could be
in that song
not for me
but for someone else
who might be
I
read
that the
Hadron Collider
can take four million pictures a second
and can bend the laws
of physics better
than Yuri Geller
can bend a spoon,
surely the eye of some god
this machine
even though prosthetic
the old women swear
by titanium knees
and carbon fiber ball joints
This age is truly a wonder.

All those scientists looking
at the splattered particles
the elusive boson among them

that confirms
some kind of glue
that accounts for
mass in space.
I do not know what
they are talking about
particles careening everywhere
we could be just that on some other
scale a pinhead
teeming infinitesimally small.

The very idea that
you live beyond
the integrity of particles
like IZZY
his ashes to the wind
his ashes to the sea
his ashes in celebration
of song and melody,
no amount of reduction
to dust
or particle
will keep
him from song
and Michael Bublé
knows this.

When Birnam Wood Walks on Two Feet

The morning reprises itself a role
stained with dawn dust illuminating the garbled misprisions
those hexen warts and all sing
as if lamplighters making their rounds
on a moonless night,
not a single plain word yet
in sight
not a single eligible bachelor thought
that might wed
and bring forth life
of some kind.
The Great Birnam wood in all this
stands sentinel before it makes its way to
high Dunsinane, shifting its centipede weight
from ambulatory leg to leg this forest scrambles
caught in a damp crevasse startled by prophecy.

The witches see
in their rhyme this and more
they have fun
their witch's Walpurgis and mal predictions
child's play
leaping like flames on the Brocken
the night hiding the facial warts the exhausted hair
the nights vibrato
wobbles and gyres
rotates and tilts
gurgle gurgle
boil burgle they steel
themselves for the full fury

of casual prophecy
slung at the disguised misfortunes
misguided Fortuna and her sisters
waiting to crawl to high Dunsinane
the trees grumble their leaves shine
they succeed in the role they play
and bring Macbeth to his knees.

The Baron Samedi

There is mud you can eat in Haiti
trucked in and mixed with
vegetable oil and rancid dreams
drunk with rum steeped in 21 peppers.

In Haiti you can taste the voodoo, Baron Samedi
pulling at the cotton in his nose telling glutton jokes
and tipping his hat he fairly dances
the smells of Cité Soleil
stanched by witflows of grief,
pepper in the ears of those who otherwise eat
street stew charcoal and garbage
a black chicken leg that dangles between the loa and every mouth.

Mudcakes! The loa Samedi smiles,
looks north and sees mountains
scaly with forest eczema
ravines where the firmament fails.

In Haiti they line up at the clinic door
and peek left and right to avoid
the Baron's grin
they shield their faces and watch soccer on cell phones
that are never hungry.

This land of prowl and broken backs
at the top and center everyone wants to be Samedi
in Haiti and wear
a tuxedo
a top hat
a grin

that captures evil
and feeds the gods
to keep them strong, at least
the Azaca loa eats
in a corner in secret
while they eat
mudcakes
in the sunlight.

The Baron Samedi finds it funny and lies
down for a rest.

Polyphemos

Oh skew-eyed chewer
of chunk-sized men
in bleating crag's camphorous damp,
sheep-chic and wooly,
your dung-crammed fingernails shy
I recall
you were the weight of one moist eye tearing
at the crusty corners where bruised vision
spotted the hairless polyphonics,
the belly-clingers, Polyphemus
cloistered inches from your kind touch
gliding from moment to gelatinous moment
in wool-stained dark
numerous voices morganatic.

A melt
For the party orb, "noman," I said
sunk that stump of fire-sick matter
coming to the point matter of factly, I listened
siren-deaf to the quiet searing in your speechless retina
one last Cyclopean focus through the splintered anxiety,
the ash and cinders, the smell
of burning mutton-fed eye.

Not knowing how to thank me, Old friend
you waved, I recall,
and flung the weight of love seaward
in a high arc,
your large man's throat
swallowing large man's tears—
the salty splash that nearly sank us both.

Sea at Mollendo

Like a phantom with a spit curl
roiling, mumbling, gyrating
this Moche sea breathes offshore through a thick
and cold phlegm—a croup that rattles in the lungs
and spews mist from the tumbling troughs
where the sea birds in gyre
ride the Humboldt current dark
and graven in the greyest of urgency
it gathers in the black canyons at depth
where conversation grins with alien teeth
and chides with scolding iridescence
the otherness of despair.

Life lacks common sense
the Moche in their dark world
lacking what looks like grace
or humor yet the bones lay in a comic heap
on the desert floor, this desiccated Eden
of jaguar teeth and spider gods
tumi and the gush of oxygenated blood
to appease suburban gods—monsters
with broad smiles and bloated heads.

Elsewhere but not far off
the turf unrolls and washes
the feet of the pre-Incan clean
with Mists that rise and float
above the plain ossified with the scribble
of cut and mutilated bone.

They see themselves
in Al Paec his untoward appetites
eight-armed, his words inky
with deception, he finds the desert
droll this octopus god.

Their cleverness with gold and copper
green and red parrot feathers,
with ceramics and textiles notwithstanding,
these preincaicos in their copper-colored enthusiasms
and iridescent evils bend and break
in sloughs of cessation no god finds satisfying.

In Huaca de la Luna land—Cajamarca
the Moche still watch
the waves that break and exhaust
their small excesses.
The sea this day its teeth
stained grey with coca, fatigue, and fear
does not smile
but argues in the deep channels and offshore valleys
the unseen movement—the hortatory violence
that remains unrecompensed.

I never feared the sea
until I came to Mollendo
the land of the Moche
and felt the mist
and saw the grey

and heard the water,
the rip tides tearing at the heart
of things
and in the back seat of the station wagon
that nearly rolled into the desert
on the way to Mollendo,
saw firsthand how finality can look with sandy eyes
through a girl's unruly bangs hiding
the funny face of the decapitator god.

Amortization

It will amortize over time,
pay down bit by bit
that large coin
of ambiguous sentiment—
love and lassitude, borrowed and banked,
ready to jump ship.

An offshore bank smiles
Giaconda, coy and intriguing
in principle deferring
the price of love, a futures commodity
selling it off with alacrity and a percentage,
merely an arithmetic algorithm,
the man with the bloated face explains.
He pushes the pen to sign,
no need to read
it's all boilerplate stuff anyway
his puffy eyes water,
his breath smells of litigation.

You offer your heart but arrogate your soul
as the song goes
and in the end pay the debt
three or four times over.

You pin the amortization schedule on the pantry wall
as if a prom date reminder
where it stays year after year
beneath the times
for garbage pickup
and recycling—the memoir
you never thought you would write.

Novalis

I sat down
at 5 PM our town
a single buzz, a lawnmower
slinging bee sounds side to side
a cloud rose high
in a towhead sky capped by a bouffant
welling above like a French fop
all edgy in gold and excess.

I sat back in my chair
the air of time ripe for Poetry
although I do not like poetry that much
I do like taking the time,
to borrow Fichte's *I*,
and throw it in the air to see
if it obeys the laws of intellectual gravity
and if so send a note to god with a wink
protesting there is too much *I* in poetry—
the wrong kind of *I* that floats
when it should sink
that masquerades as a toddler god
gaga-gooing, throwing up food
strewing creation here and there
as if in a tantrum.

For my part I will relax my grief,
resume bickering with those gods
dead and dying,
Sophie staring from the threshold wondering
if she looks ok if she looks

pretty enough to die romantic
if her petticoat and shoes and bonnet will bring me to tears
she lies there noting I am not paying attention per se,

I have another Sophie on my mind, gosh,
I think
she's dead!

They say I locked the door
and scored the bedpost
and told her I was she
and she was I, which sounds odd in the past tense.
I buried her with good tears and swore to follow
and Christianize this deadbeat god once and for all,
and drag him back to finish the magic,
to poeticize the night
to take care of his casually begotten kids.

Finally, I said with good cheer and balance,
the kind moral ballast gives,
I was not afraid of death
as much as I was afraid of love.

My horse saggy in the middle
much like my thoughts
on the matter, I ride
towards imperturbable finality
at its own pace and humor.

Sophie waits for me on the Other side
still stuttering,
tepid of mind and soul
waiting
for someone
to give her a hand-held mirror.

The Global Seed Vault

In the global seed vault
not a single beach body stirs
in seed form, of course, they wait
dreaming of never ending
spring and carpeting the broken earth with colorful life.

They dream beyond the fears
that put them there
in the inky dark, locked away
as if a collective Antigone paying
for an act that is neither
sin nor valor.

There they talk of the Hindu Kush,
what they will do when the sensi seeds bloom
and the sandalwood comes to life
and the charas and the saffron flower
in the valleys of the Pamir
whisper ancient promises and vow an ancient love
that has no name.

Penthesilea

Your little feet patter
pitter with danger your eyes far sharper
than the arrows you sling.

Outrageous you throw me back
like a snot-nosed trout too small
to grill—this
catch and release love—
new to me!

I don't understand
your middle name unnecessarily calibrated
in Epos and Simulacrum

Our battles are local you know,
not large.
Our sieges, flip
and whiny, no need
for vast armies.

The ballistae and trebuchets we have rolled in place
to fight I shake my head
this emotion so heavy to sling?

The siege guys shuffle and laugh—
no walls to breach,
no glory to win,
they mill about,
bad smelling, dirty, skew-eyed
and in the end watch the myth come crashing down,
more like Jericho than Troy.

Not to cast blame, my empty ballista empty, you launched
yourself into that specious air like a Hollywood stunt gal,
doing your own tricks
and like a George Romero zombie
all druggy and grey-eyed, terrified me with dead love
lurching without end.

You shot an arrow through my throat
which, while rude, gives me an idea
how to bring Hector to his patellae
in a future fiction.

Awaiting your Word I have a friend
who is convinced that she can travel,
powder burns and all, alone
and her name too is Penthesilea,
as Amazonian as you but terminally ill yet
she wants to make a death pact
which takes love too far . . .

I have a task at hand
while my larynx still works
I will speak to you prophetic
as Priam spoke to Hektor:

"No dogs will be your comfort;
Penthesilea, it's your party
you can cry if you want to."

Facebook Meditation

Depending on point of view,
you or I will draw a last breath
and move a final bowel inadvertently
by way of saying both hi and bye
somewhere down the road of finite time,
and in this ochred and watery dusk
with heavy eyes and unspoken regrets
will wonder briefly how
a countable moment gives way
to uncountable rest.

On the chair with the button that raises
one high and then tips one forward to stand up,
at reluctant attention,
on this chair
below this chair
in this chair
toenail parings and popcorn kernels
in fused and tattered ecumenical order,
tell the tale as a saga redacted—
shrunk to the size of a small portal,
a dime-size circle of dim light
sniffing at the edge of darkness
like an old hound unable to find the scent of return.

The last countable breath
will make the sound of pop and ping—
no whisper no gasp no sigh
just the click of a broken part ungearing
the rasp of a jagged heartbeat stuck
in soft linkage flux.

On this day of blessed travel,
whatever you hold onto to by way of wag or wish
will shake the dogged belief back and forth
and make of heaven a poor man's lunch,
the statal authority
of every pious Christian
and every devout Muslim
who says to you, *ah poor Other*
as they parse your sins and wave you off
to purgatory or *Barzakh*
or kill you outright for your own good.

Magician's Hubris

It drifts through us
like a mist, a small cloud, a murky overcast.
Neither father that abandons family
nor mother who slips away down those back steps of longing
can colonize despair like IT does.
This monogamous sleight-of-hand,
what kind of trick is this?
When revealed we say:
How Simple
How Clever
How Awful
the night that shills for absent grace and rises
and fills like the waters of a great lock
slowly
inexorably
wantonly
until one day in dream's flight
the fancymonger cries *wolf in the breast!*
and legerdemain takes
father mother brother and sister
as the magician takes
a bow.

A Sea of Other (Redux)

I.   Not a moment to lose, the rivets popping
        like rivets do under stress
        along the bulkhead they run and taper,
        this romance no match
        for the addered stuff under the water waiting—

        On the deck in the jeweled dark
        celebrity ice scatters and drives the saline sky
        back into the sea.
        "It is pointless."
        "We're doomed!"
        They wink and nod and lob the cryptic cold at each other
        while below it tears, unzips
        the flawed marital skin.
        Above, the music plays on
        and night coagulates
        as melody thins
        as love bleeds out . . .

II.   Elsewhere a small difference in body parts
        hides a crucial otherness: he squirms and tumbles
        head over heels, his eternal feminine huddles
        into the lifeboat that sways with ambivalent disapproval
        as the other *other* watches from above.

        His transgender decision deepens the distress--
        sickened by fear and manliness he opts
        to remain buoyant and hides his she-face from heroism,
        while under frosty stars Love stiffens in the arctic air,
        arches and plunges to unforgiving depths,
        a breakup that groans in the dark
        while tiny things all around
        bob and flail and slip
        into a sea of other.

Dolan

"...There would be no story without the scenes that interrupt it."
"Hit Men," by Clive James (concerning Peter Bogdanovich)

"Dolan should have dressed down
for this occasion,"
the tiny voice squeaks
still humming the names of Trojan clans
at the swift running queries
of Gigantic Diomedes
and Cunning Odysseus
gun for him . . .

"Am I body
or do I have a body?"
A philosopher's thought
in bridal carapace—

Giant Diomedes
Cunning Odysseus
notice the epic chic
the grey wolf pelt
and mottled marten's cap
Dolan's wedding best.

Bricolage sinks into the night—
Chat gone clerical in the Trojan dust.

Gigantic Diomedes
Cunning Odysseus
dogs of death
mark their territory,
repatriate this vexillary of ambition,
redress his sartorial muchness with ambush.

They sniff him thoroughly,
this old dog of war,
the otherwise man of gold and bronze
not enough it seems
for him this night
Dolan mans these handlers
with blind oars on a mad sea
despairs within deaf earshot of the black-prowed ships.

Blushing he swears
Hector is a coward and a bully
and daubs himself in eager tones
of ransom, inchoate pleas drift
off to the Dardanelles.

Gigantic Diomedes
Cunning Odysseus
buzz at him like so many flies
on a week-old carcass,
question him to death.

He likes the Achaean attention
betrays Hector time and again
until cutting edge technology
dissociates for real
that sensibility Dolan quizzes.
Slung in the dust,
he ponders their crude answer
the pitiless bronze that asseverates
the small truth.

"Rude Achaeans,"
he thinks and thinks stuck
matrimonially in small thought,
not exactly a body
nor possessing a body exactly . . .
Their eyes strut and follow the curves of his question
the dead head
unable to give up speech . . .

Thought passes
already slurred by the lapping
black water
his marten's cap pulled down jauntily
the trireme's eye moist with joy—
it gives Dolan away
to the night.

Kaukalin (Kaukauna)

The skull of chief Weyauwega sits on a shelf
at the Smithsonian waiting for return
to the "resting place" — the coasts of Weyauwega
wild with thorn brush and cranberry.
It tilts its gaze upward
next to the dried spleen of an old lion
that died at the edge of the Serengeti
and the Incan child, nose stuffed with coca leaves,
her arms folded in mummified prayer.

Kaukauna too has its dry gild
that gleams Homeric,
the Indian rhapsode always inventing,
the namer of things epic and not, wandering
up and down the Fox River,
a Johnny Appleseed of fine words
spoken in fine syllables he says:
Here—the resting place.
and in performance pitch and waver
Here—the place to catch the pickerel.
He barely passes the proficiency exam
yet names everything in sight,
searching the Season's worth
in grim attenuation and flaccid words like we all do,
searching for the place of return
with loopless wit and tonsured spirit.

Yet, these slotted loyalties to literature and life drain him,
leave him wordless and wondering if it is enough
to name the place of pooled pike
to name them trapped
in another kind of return. Meanwhile,

half an unknown planet away the Chumash on their rounded island
in Santa Barbara Bay
pot around in parsimonious philosophies,
keeping their gods few and their women plump.
With facility and joy they build canoes and trade and call this
worship—
for the sake of the Europeans
who feel it is a universal impulse
to prostrate oneself and pray
to one's weakness and disloyalties.
Like Weyauwega sitting on a shelf,
the Chumash in their bad clothes and Edenic swagger
wink at each other
and say to these iron-covered Spanish,
the sometimes fearers of god:
Welcome to our world
filled to the brim with small distractions.
Trade you our chubby women for some beads?

In *Kaukalin* near the shores of Winnebago
the French claim their continent
paddling downriver, practicing their declarations
of eminent domain.
The Indian poet
unschooled in legalese
unable to mount an argument instead
renames the seven-day world he knows—
the partings and pain
the births and deaths
the loves and regrets
that tumble down the waterfall every spring

while Allouez and La Salle,
Marquette and Hennepin
apply the poultice and camphor,
the analgesic insentience of religion and greed
the Indian poet fails to feel.

The creak of wagon wheels brings
commerce and wiggly viri to kill them off
where the pike progress from year to year
and snap and bicker how best to die
in the pools beneath the place where the river drops.
There the afternoon sun can drip like honey
and suffocate with sadness the barely thought through
emotion of living . . .

Ascending the back steps on the side of the rental
I remember my aunt and uncle, the sulphur
in the air and sky and churches
in their lungs and moments of love.
I remember Kaukalin as a place to gather
on ransom day when someone in the
crowd will barter it all for a trinket's song
and *Gau Gau Ning's* peripatetic poet laureate
will find his homely words and declare:

Here, the place of blinking eyes.

Apple John's Lament

I am a corn-sick Apple-John
my wares wobble and wiggle,
waggle and wish
me to squire them to this grim stop-over.
We have our arrangements we like to think
we choose, my big toe sick with gout
an angnagle sprouting its nail head
evolving only a few consonants at a time
becoming a frayed and irritating hangnail—the spirit in me
nothing less than a common fester.

My Eves of dinge and apple sores bought and sold
have received their Swarovski manicure sets I'm told
and in that time before and after
legs akimbo serpentine charm still fresh as dew,
they trim and file and resolve at dusk
that Eden will never do.

Loser

I bury failure often and with some tears
the recent poetry contest winner an exception.
I snort simpering poetic maledictions—
wrong words that slash at him possibly her
with the blunt intent to shatter and bash
to bury either one or both in bad reviews.

I haven't won a poetry contest yet
the problem is that
I am driven to step to the podium and deliver
an encomium to myself that sounds
like the slather of snake oil on dry skin that
can't be softened—
the problem is that
my soul's desiccated with an off-brand envy.

I fall asleep and exhale stupid air
a droll drool bubble drips down my chin,
a bed-head script that says:

"I will freeze you in a bad quatrain
possibly plagiarize and then misquote,
abuse your words and with laughter
steal your daughters and then
go home
and tend this herpes sore."

Like Rasputin, words and intrigue stuck in his beard,
eyes reddened by Mesmer and Hypnos
I will draw you in powerless
and with criminal generosity
pan your dismal words,

you dreamers of drivel
you brokers of poetic universals boasting meaning
in the flight of a bee or loss of a shirt button.

That skinny guy possibly gal just won the poetry contest
like that, as if the world were contained
in a drop of acid rain . . .
He/She had a picture ready for the occasion—
that is hubris of a high order
punishable by shunning or ceaseless recitation
to an audience of high schoolers
the occasion for them a floating Island
of egotism for sure
dagnammit, Brobdingdagnammit
I swear for effect, my loss
systemic and rheumatoid,
rehearsed and scripted.

There is an ice cream sandwich waiting
for me
for occasions like this
for consolation I keep it in the freezer
next to those who have looked me in the eye / I
to those who have left in search of the transcendent.

I am beside myself
on this day of poetic misery
unable to find the alchemy that can
change this small dross into a precious metal
that has some cash value.

Breakfast at Penelope's

Breakfast need not be compliant.
I don't see why this jacket has patched elbows sewn with leather
as if I were an asymmetrical crustacean crawling ashore
as I may have done in Phaeacia—
to shore
to love
to war,
that over, I lecture
seeking solace, breakfast not the place to say:
"I long to raid . . ."

I cannot tell Her this,
still wrapped in the scent of Ogygian perfume,
but I long
to grasp the sword and smell the sea,
I need crime and criminal love,
Scylla and Charybdis
some coffee and desire and breath
to understand You.

Why do you continue to wait for Him?
He's gone there's only Me
Please,
pass the goat cheese.

Poetry Class (Ostranenie— "Making Strange")

A poem comes
every so often
like a thief in the night or a postman in the day
when most robberies and deliveries occur.

Like an unwanted child on your doorstep
helpless and hungry and whiny . . .

"All clichés, of course"
the tired poet says
"All clichés which batter
the door of poetry
and threaten the frightened meaning inside
again and again
with a deadness that has the head of a ram
and the body of a large tree limb."

"The poetry is next door," he says.
Early on an October morning
when leaves are crisp and colorless
and the dark smells of cinnamon and cider remain
aloof to the perennial and overstated pain of living,
here is where the poetry happens,
when the dispute between night and day
resolves itself in a gloaming
that fidgets with faith and hope.

And so her window shade dampens
with a frizzy florescence that mottles into grey
that ambushes the night

with hidden dayness,
a prelude to siege warfare
that throws up the dead bodies of QVC—
vegetable dicers and costume jewelry,
like defenders of Carcassonne, arching the last pig
into the sky as proof
the war could last forever . . .

The TV throws grey light into night
sends images beyond the moon
only to be snagged and dispersed,
spread and thinned like some seedless jam on soggy toast
far into deep space, her space . . ."

"There you go, that is a good start!" he says
with sanguinity and a yawn.
"Now, an allusion to epic pain,
to pathos the Greeks call it,
to Antigone recalling her goddess double shackled to a rock,
finding fear and misgiving
chained to a flower under a pastel sky."

"Question? Yes, in the back?"
"When does the cafeteria close?"
(those Russian guys call this *Ostranenie)*
"At 8 PM, I believe."

Annunciation: Vern Goslin

Apart from your prayers
I do not exist
like you think, I do I am
merely what you have prayed for
nothing before or after me
the efficacy of prayer surprises
me more than you I am
in your service and aim to please.

That is why angels and devils both
have wings . . .

Well thanks and nice to see you
let me say nothing writes as well
as on this parchment this thinnest of skins no wonder
we tat our bodies write ourselves
the way we do unable to imagine
we are anything but comic book characters
with so little to say
and this surface ink stammering to say it.
Most holy books are like that
so don't feel bad.

Rather its erasure I seek a way out
waiting let's say,
for a better message
for a campy story
for a messiah whose appetite
for suffering is meatless I'm waiting
for a messenger like you,
preferably sent from the sky

still downy white, a little chubby
with ruddy cheeks but with traces of adult acne.

This is what I prayed for:
someone who could have fallen from heaven
and survived
whose allegiance is gauged by the ether miles pedaled
between heaven and hell
between hope and despair.

I have prayed for a message
with teledramatic stops,
delivered by a messenger
who smiles and salutes,
who wears a jaunty bell-boy cap
and puffs out his chest,
a message etched on bureaucratic parchment
that claims to know wise rivers
that carve and layer our geologies of self
into headstrong religions
that claim to take us home.

Tell me the good news that you float not fly,
that you were tempted to tell Him off like them,
that heaven is better than hell, but not by much.

You know,
You remind me of Vern Goslin—
This ain't yer first rodeo, either,
and this ain't the first time
you been throwd out of heaven.

The Language of Valentine's Day

We have a little light
to show us for a while
the way
a gritty light that has dissolved color
into a grey wave of fade and fatuity—

       …romanticism is nothing
       but a kind of exponentiation . . .

The giveaway on Valentine's Day
is the Otherness we guard with ignorance
and curiosity, a language
we cannot speak it sounds like the bleat
of time (if it were sheep)

       "Nature has in the human spirit
       broken through to consciousness itself
       and its active powers . . ."

I wish I had those Nat Geo reptile eyes
that go up and down, in and out
back and forth, this way and that
to watch for the coming of the Great Other
bound to appear anytime now
looking for insects, hungry to eat.

I cannot understand life lodging
the way it does somewhere between
extravagant and plaintiff,
excessive and desperate just to say

look at me as if the plea
of a needy god uncertain and alone
afraid you'll say: "Let's just be friends."

Close to noon on this love celebratory day,
I hide in the shadowless middle and wait
to hear the sun step into a little darkness
and promise return as it does.

There is little difference
between promises and fears
light and darkness for all that.
A friend rises from his sickbed
to say as much,
sees a tree standing upright and thinks
the Lear thought:
Why should a dog or horse or rat have life . . .?
but then concludes why not?

      To take command of the transcendental self . . .

He spits, rinsing his mouth of prayer—
how things thrive
with pointless purpose and complex unities,
the tiniest of life sparks,
jammed deep into the hard stuff of stupid creation.

On this Valentine's day
I cannot help but feel old and abstract
brokered and bought
tinkered and tampered with
standing here on the side of the Road
going Elsewhere listening, while
hitching a ride with an opposable thumb.

Meno: A Beauty Unmenaced
(Iota in the Afterlife)

I have discovered for the first time I
should say recovered the eristic breath of Meno
and now believe that
the tree and the flower
the sun and the moon
the alpha and omega
have been mine all along.
I forget here in Ohio how much I know
of virtue and soul, of *Eros* and *Agape*.

I dine at the house of Agathon,
the epideictic chatter between bites of dolmades
loud, the talk of virtue and goodness, strange
ideas I do not need on my trip—I look to Osiris
consolations I know in my pharaoh's life—
cosmogonic sex or sipping Tenenit's beer
some emmer wheat and figs.

These mounted thoughts like Nubian horsemen
scare me yet accompany me on my Journey
down darkly colorful corridors
dug with ferret teeth beneath sandstone I am cheered
at the clink and clank of my trove
my clunky numbers melted into geometric ingots
of orphic wisdom, my arithmetic coffin filled
with jostling Mnemosyne they bury

me with my sacred numbers
so I can speak the langue of the life to come
and chat with a god or two . . .
You see it's true—
You can take it with you.

The Basel Nightingale

A musty turn of heart
no nightingale, however
sweet its song
will sing
of *annates* or *expectatives* or *precaria*
that dwell in the breach
between *Ohrmazd* and *Ahriman.*

In their factories of contention
these thinking woodcutters split
the soulish thing its flesh from bone,
flense the spirit then recede slinking
into dirty cowls and holy hoodies,
gangsters hiding in transubstantiations
of stone and tree, wine and water,
the benefices of self-loathing and proud piety,
they are the first to harvest the low hanging fruit
already rotting on the Tree.

We pray for belief
and for the day
when we no longer need to suffer
the logic of redemption
or the ecstasy of renunciation
and from the Venusberg or Brocken
look to enjoy the full cacophonous melody
of a god waking
to the human Other
curious and coy asking
"What *are* your *Names, dear ones*?"

Indictment

You candlewaster quack
You kobold with a pen
selling amulets and glass beads
pretty cloth and ribbons
to unwary sinners—innocents
foreswunke in lists of philanthropy and to-do.

Superior in their devout enthusiasms
and religious arts, they buy up
your salves and ointments
and Philosopher's Eggs by the dozens
nested in bright but fatal inquiry
and like the *salvor* who tastes for a living
hope "not today."

They apply this poultice,
these fatty philistines and armchair patriots
and sink in viral comfort to wait . . .

They recall the amber nights,
the times when they manned and womanned the barricades
high atop the trundled palaver and ergonomic philosophies
of the sacral *Self* from here they slung
their taunts and sneers from the makeshift obstacle
thinking it might endure or thwart
that body of empty stabilities waiting ten deep
to butcher up their heroisms.

And there they take their stand
at someone else's rebellion
brave and happy to have been called
to the higher *Self,*

eager for otherworldly recompense
and the gaud of heavenly casinos, the gilded spas
that echo with grace
as redemption appears sail-first on the horizon
only to sail away.

Orange County Cruiser

In Isla Vista
no one takes vows of obedience
celibacy, or significance
without first riding to the sea.

I listen in vain for the drift of morning matins
but hear instead the click of a single gear
against the sound of lapping waves—
I hear the rollers open
to the drive sprocket—mechanical love-making
of a kind that poets celebrate.

I'm one with this Orange County Cruiser—
Half man, half bike—a centaur
fused and ready for unbridled mischief . . .
On the other hand it is
a way of simplifying the day without recourse
to Zen mindfulness or garbled philosophy.

I mount this clunky bike like everyone else
in a moment of morning love
free from the Shimano complexities of shifting gears
or the bullying torque of wrenching religion.
I pedal with the easy rythmn of nature-faith—
the ups and downs
of niveau flexibilité or existential étiquette
absorbed by the zeppelin tires
half-filled with stale air.

When to go easy, when to go hard
takes up only a small space
where the maids of *moira* weave and measure and cut
the single thread, the single speed is enough
to allow me to linger in morning light and quiet,
where the soft bells of veiled truth are seen and heard.

In this world getting around
is no easy matter
one must don sackcloth and pray
against one's will,
watch at crossings, heed the traffic.

One must postulate and repudiate
the planet's spin and gyre
and join a cloister or a monastery
where protective walls and regular meals prove god's special love.

This Orange County cruiser
its muscled cuirass retro and defiant,
speaks the language of unintended prayer—
the language of promise unfulfilled
the language of dream and reverie.

I pedal the Orange County cruiser down
Embarcadero to the sea
past the surfer rentals and sorority houses
where the cliff gives way to the wind and water,

and ask myself why Greek Anaximander believed
that the unchanging center of things might be proven,
that redemption of earth, water, air and fire
lay with the math waiting to be done.

Thinking how the Pythia playing with her curls
sat in the *adyton* vaping as the kids do now,
omphalos-centered and awful pretending
to know the gods through smoke and babble
makes me wonder elsewhere
how Benedict came up with the rule
that to live, one must pray and work.

An Orange County cruiser
does not drive itself
or come to its own conclusions
about the unmoving center of things.
It does not utter hallucinogenic prophecy
or obey monastic rule for that matter,
nor does its chain often derail.

Elpenor

Without some loss of sleep
under cross-eyed stars and cypress gaze
drunk and dreaming Elpenor
tumbles
falls in febrile steepness
off the witch's roof.

First to uncrumple him great Odysseus:
"Your neck's broken," he says eyes akimbo,
"No flatter a warrior's fate anywhere."

Already Elpenor unwept and unburied
stands on his tiptoes looking
for Charon on that dark river,
he hears
Shade laughter on the opposite shore
and futzes red and rumpled
with a lament that plays
at his fingertips—
he pleads to anechoic faces:
"Plant my oar upright"
and stumbles into Hades
a standup-hero
in modern times—
an upright oar
neither sound in mind,
nor powerful in body
but bold
in blameless mediocrity.

A Station of the Cross (the Thief to the Left)

"Boxed into badness,
narrow shoulders and all,
too far along for redemption,"
his voice slivers and falls
from the high purview of retrospect wisdom,
I can say it is a not a special cross I bear
rather it bears me—a slab of raw sinner
hung high for all to see. And you?

"Thanks for asking, but if I may—
you sell yourself short as if
there is no return on the set-aside
you thought would double
your cachet in this rust-belt world.

I'm coming back to make things right
I promise you, but if I may—
You can't live off the legacy of shifting Sin forever;
nor live in the prophet's basement thinking life
will get better—don't mean to be preachy
but look down there.

Your mother is crying, all pudgy and broken
worn out with despair
steeped in that sorrow that has foreign words
no one understands
and spreads like oil atop muddy water—
Not to make you feel bad,
I want to point out
my mom too! There beneath me watching

oh, the pain I have put her through
if only she knew the clouds will part.
We will all go home soon.

"Boxed into badness," my friends still say
But why are You so calm today?

The world from up here, an empty mall
an abandoned factory, dilapidation all
the junk along the way
this via dolorosa, will get worse
before it gets better,
but I am set on return
will fix these roads
and gentrify these neighborhoods
with the kind of grace that greens the grass
and shines forth in painted clapboard.
I will expiate that albatross-Sin that hangs
around your neck
and redeem the deplorables, milling beneath us
now it is time
to get you out of the basement . . .

See how their eyes measure
each shrug and fall
of our narrow shoulders,
but die assured you will always be
the thief to My left
whose friendly chat and dry lament
construed as sorrow for sin
will win you heaven. Say, this
is beginning to hurt!

What About the Roman Guy?

On the day of resurrection
the nameless dog fails
to rise the Roman guy stands
nonetheless at cave's mouth, wet breath damp
it's spring outside Golgotha
garlanded in *raqefeth* and *dam hamakabin*
the leather of his sandals cracked, dusty
crisp and legible like leaves yes in Haifa's fall.

He's tired and yawny
mangy and far away from home.
"They kill them crazy here"
 he thinks, "as if taking apart Legos,"
the sleep stuff melting
in the corners of his eyes.
"Why don't they just let them
hope and love, believe and talk?"
ripples outward on the surface of morning
gray and green and pink
the colors of Jerusalem in spring.

The sun rises the rooster crows
actually, and really.
The Roman guy's mom wants to know
if it's cold in Jerusalem, if his sandals are worn,
if the olives are good, if his tunic is torn the blood
of the Maccabees pink this morning after.

The cave breathes a sigh,
He is gone or risen or stepped out
for a moment,
a fluttery shroud, a swirly vortex
shimmers in the morning air,
a Love he just begins to see.

Varangian Angels

They bob and weave
dodge and dance around
those already gone the Decembrist rebels
who had been many degrees real
and several inches thick
with life when they left,
the idea lingered as they receded
into the past these Varangians
selling themselves to the stars,
to the strongest god who needed them
and needs them still
to wage petty wars of gimme
to keep seraglios of earthy spawn
safe from those katechons of
want otherwise dedicated
to simple greed—the rapacity
of locusts emerging after years of sleep.

They left as light
already dim but fell
glowing, spewing comet ire and threats,
drooling clouds of discontent through space
they come to rest
bitter but bold still,
their powerful muscles pulsate,
their toe tips and finger tips tingle,
livers and pancreas girths swell as the last rays arrive
with news the second coming is not likely.

They will fight
and find the place of easy death
and smash His face and scatter His teeth
and watch His eyes bulge wherever they find Him,
the shape-shifting Antichrist
and reclaim their place thinking
"either way we lose."

Time to gather the broad axes and bent shields
lick our wounds and smooth our feathers
Time to go home.

Pulling Pints: the First Christmas

Pulling pints three wise men
tend the bar, far Magi
who rule the night, the light
of one small star
long since dead
watching the foamy sky rise
to the glass' wide edge.

They wait
to top it off
with faith and hope, prayer and love—
some kind of redemption sudsy with belief
that fills the stable, like fog that fills a valley
that fills the dustup dogma to the brim, like traders yelling
as stocks dip and plunge.

It lay chubby and mercantile this Child
in scripted night
in scripted manger.

The small human artifact wondrous and rosy
but prickled and rashy beneath the accomplished twinkling
of eyes and stars,
Single shafts of straw
Single sprigs of thistle
drawing the warmth away.

It lay in desert-cold catechism
a froth atop a dark brew.

In their eyes moistened by the smell of camel dung and desert cold,
they mount the question
how dead light might travel so far and accomplish so much
and the night's dark foam
running down the sides of galaxies
collapsing right and left.

They lean back in dromedary chic
and watch the sky
and wager that the star will speak
that the heavens will open
in a single word that
will streak across the horizon
they bet that
following the star
that brings so much talk will announce
a messiah of circumspection who
will cut the heavens in two with a comet's flash.

They look each other in the eyes,
and donkey and dog and lowing cow,
diorama beasts sensible and shy,
grin piously as dead light shrieks and cuts the
multiverse in multiples of twos!

Oh to see that sign
and feel the great joy . . .
to smell the frankincense and
myrrh charming the gold into
pixie dust!

Their crowns settle deep into their royal skulls,
they say: "Let's go home
and drink a beer and eat buffalo wings.
Let's watch the game and maybe
just maybe the star, if ignored, will not die
and the child, if ignored, will not live."

The Persian King's Dog

I want to be loved by something
large and living
with friendly canine teeth
that can tear flesh and enliven a snarl.

I want to be loved by something that has poor memory
and excusable bad habits,
that licks its wounds and procreative parts
with democratic equanimity
as if claiming pedigree,
as if some Persian King's mastiff
entitled to indulge calumny and slobber,
infidelity and silence at will.

Fawning aside, breathing at my feet will do.

The Brief Life (Notes on an Art Gallery Visit)

The convex language of a seamless bubble speaks
to me its surface tension an exotic sound
that wobbles toward my ears
in the key of burst and bust.

The moment reprises a pastel rainbow
and the oily beauty of a time
of giant ferns and armored crabs.

I've seen this before
heard it sung
differently—this complicated beauty
curved and levitating,
unlikely to survive its wet roundness
it will pop and you will wonder
where did it go?

The Gerber Viper

"You will never know the regret
that comes and goes with failure
to buy the Gerber Viper
1.6 liter gpf commode,"
the guy said as if a prophet just washed ashore
selling a new religion out of the back of his car.
"Commodious," he said
"You will never regret your Gerber Viper,"
and showed me how
it swallowed 3.5 lbs. of baby carrots
as if Jonah's whale,
which gave me pause.
He said, "Sit on the Viper,"
which required some faith on my part
"Let me know how it feels."

"Kinda like a LazyBoy, but the name has me concerned,"
I said and wondered if this proselytizer
had recently fallen off a horse
and now had me in his sights as a practice convert.
I nod and acknowledge his beatnik god
who commandeers great whales
to swallow disbelievers whole and flush them
through doctrinal baleen as easily as flushing
3.5 lbs of baby carrots down the Gerber Viper,
I convert. He says: "Enjoy the throne!"
which I did and do like a Borgia pope
without shame or complication.

And in the future as sins vary in kind and number,
I will try flushing 3.5 lbs. of broccoli florets
to test the claims of this religion of inclusion,
and bring myself to talk of the Gerber Viper
in tones of liberation theology and neocatechumenal joy.

The Flesh of Diomedes

Every arrow
passes clean through me my flesh
butter and cream no broad barb
stops to mourn . . .

I throw my spear it arcs and misses.
I trot to pick it up thinking
some bodacious bowman is looking
me up and down to perforate me
the thigh
the shoulder
the foot
as if death needs some help
to wrest from me some grace
some humility
some mortality misused.

I find this odd—
the Troad so dusty,
my twisted thumbs useless
to decipher these gods
my soul too weary
to take comfort in glory,
the large word Death so small.

The Venus of Willendorf
(the Shopping Cart Lady)

In that flimsy part of the sky
she held to, she clutches the royal purple
barely big enough to get round
her tummy—a little bubble-chubby
with some god's kid.
She whispers as the grocery cart wheels jamb
and swivel and make that thunder
that echoes in her head.
The sky belches, the traffic lights change
the final coming not so apocryphal
she rubs her stomach what kind of world
will it know?

Against white phyllo clouds buttery and blue
her fructified self grows,
the hands of amateur sculptors
choking the clay,
announcing her homelessness,
they set her on the altar
where she holds
the sky in one hand
the earth in the other.

Her face pocked and sunken,
her teeth grey and missing,
she bends under the weight of a *katechon*
holding back mindless regressions,
twists and turns, the garble
left by indigent antichrists
held in abeyance

until the Time comes.
They look her up and down
at the checkout recoiling.

She cannot see her feet,
can't be sure
she is touching ground.
She grows heavy with ellipsis
and the reverence of ignorant others
waiting for her blessing.

She wanders off into herself
as ancient gods often do,
clutching food stamps in one hand
referral forms in the other,
knowing it is good to keep friends close
but better to keep one's godhead closer.

The universe
assigns her a number; she waits
large with miraculous child,
raw with love she wonders
if the Father will send
his only son or daughter,
if the tender *childmignon*
in its place of *divine procession*
will ever come
to know Him.

Bumblebee

There is a black and yellow bumblebee
out there amid the purple cinerarias,
still technically unable to fly
but not concerned as it might be.
Pollen-sleepy, its bumblefur
dusted bright in sunlight,
it bobs and bumps in flight
from purple to purple
pollen-drunk and frizzy-eyed.

Inches from this fuzzball flyer,
I recoil and recall
the terror back then I crawled
to the back window of the yellow Mercury
no deliverance, however, by the sandal-winged god,
my mother picking apples and I oedipal wanting this Eve
my way (Freud tells me).
Three bumble bees sensing perversion
sting me time and again for my honest deviance,
anechoic, my screams go unheard
as it should be with any good punishment—
no analyst needs to bill me that!
"Get over it!" they say.
"We lose our stingers, you, your bad behavior.
You will think twice next time you call up
some Freudian depravity and thank us."

Should I build a memorial to my red lumps,
militarize them with hope and resolve vowing
"never again,"

or should I wait and watch, dream and drift
and like them, rub my cutaneous wings together
and fly when the physics of Freudian love
tells me I can't?

Transition Neighborhood

This neighborhood broken
depreciating its sidewalks buckling
its windows boarded up
zoned it seems for single family despair;
it needs some upkeep.

The absentee landlord
accepts no email, returns no calls
takes no responsibility,
off somewhere flipping galaxies gone bad.
He sublets love per contract details,
"Adulation paid the first of each month."
A mortmain smelling of garbage and disrepair.

He's the same Guy who 4 am
wants to sell His knowledge
Cheap for our sake, they say
He smiles altruistic:
"You all can learn to flip houses.
I've made my fortune fixing
fixer uppers—Galaxies here and there
in bad bad neighborhoods and you can too."

What moves in after all is bought and sold
feels like earache and ingrown toenails
like heartburn and psoriasis,
smells like camphor and phlegm.

What moves out
some spring-green religion
some cathedral birds
some love like that for a pet
that has run away.

I tell myself I will stand up
to this slum-god subletting doxa,
His neighborhood in shambles,
and tell Him He needs to fix things—
a roof a gutter a window.
I will tell him
He cannot
abandon us.

I will complain about the ants and spiders
the crumbling foundations and leaky pipes,
the universe left unpainted and peeling,
and cosmic junk strewn everywhere.

I will phone and email
this Guy until He returns
my prayers.

The Soul's Last Day

(1) Emily Post will tell you
the word is wrong, belongs to another time
is puffy and effete,
like a designer dog—
an amalgam of ears, eyes, noses, and paws
created to love unconditionally
but unable to reproduce.
The soul sits in anyone's lap
crouches in moral crevasses
where it waits for His return.

(2) On some days "my soul" falls
as if a limb cut the wrong way;
it crashes down smashing everything its shadow hides
this solid specter of retribution,
of filler words congruently empty and thwarted,
ring upon ring of Bethlehemic repose
that tells of the ravage and drought—
the ice and wind of every cycle of redemption.

(3) Once I said to myself, "My soul aches."
It sounded like a cough, phlegm and all
sputum mixed with blood.
That soupy dogma never settles a stomach
already upset . . .
There is a pill I take that gives relief
and makes me want to make a commercial:
I sit on a couch with a loved one
whom I look at peppery with puppy eyes
and as she speaks the miracle of *soul,* I interrupt:

"Like others I thought this invention an invention,
like the Edsel, overhyped until I discovered . . ."
which I can never finish.

(4) The discomfort enlarges boisterously
all rubbery and willing to violate boundaries
of sacred decency, it pulses, in me, in us, in them—
a wayward allegiance to the limits of mortality
unchecked by intuition.
This sacred bloat in polite company drifts us upward
contrary to Newton et al. and rises distending all belief.

(5) But today it drifts flaccid.
I look away embarrassed, ashamed
as it puddles in sad effervescence,
a patina of hope that covers all empathy.
I look for the unhandsome face in the crowd
that glows in blighted loyalty to a faraway self,
significant and god-sponsored, the perfect rescue,
this *psyche* finds itself on rocky ground
within the pouring of night-dust
under the blanching moon it prays
at Gethsemane like other messiahs—
and despairs Human sweating blood
that drains the sacred swag.

(6) "My soul," I use the expression
like a casual girlfriend who sexes me out,
leaves me now and then fed up.
My soul flounders, stares at TV, sinks into covetousness.

She wants a family and kids, a house and three cars,
I'm not sure if I can write a psalm about that,
maybe an off Broadway hit
that begins with someone selling someone
time shares to the New Eden,
a talking face patient and shifty
well-rehearsed in the noetics of
redemption and ready to proselytize.

(7) My soul has barely an echo when it speaks
but has a scent that suggests
a floral arrangement, a *koan* fragrance
that pulpiteers share for a price
and pay down their unchristian debts
and finance their unchristian homes—
homely sacristies from which they peer
empty and cautious their bluster a little too biblical.

(8) The Psalm says "my soul is thirsty for the Lord,"
which is sound and color, pink and green and blue
It is sunrise and sunset, I get it—
as my soul, thin and skittery, flutters away incontinent.

Corfiot Mourning Dove

I fly to your bough
and alight, feeling the gentle shiver
and bend of your presence
your skin and breath
your touch and recoil
and in that instant am gone
your branches still trembling
in the morning dark.

Sardanapalus

Ods bodkins
I dare to say
it's a hot
it's a hot
it's a hot, hot day
my harem-hatched odalisque
come home to sprawl to lay
tender-thighed waste to me
someone's army
not far away . . .

You call me Sardanopolis
your hutched gaze empty
all ends at your feet
at whose wits end you've come,
I am yours . . .

How sweet of you
whose army at my door to bother
an otherwise fine day
of multiple couplings?
Ods bodkins
I dare to say
it's truly truly a hot hot day.

The Ship from Delos

Seven lions sejant
worn teeth, receding manes, tired eyes
lean
against chalk dryness and better judgment,
I bought Pepsi and souvlaki at shore's edge
the cordial Polyphemus and his protean pelican
herding us into the hold—the awkward lesson of history—
Someone's death
looming as a dot on the sea's far reach,
the risible geometry and roundness
of finality's highest point first seen
In Mykonos
where the posh crowd lingers couchant
beneath the cantilevered sky
and beer-bellied windmills.

In ship's belly
we spat up Calliope-like
philosophy and amazement
in eloquent and timeless tones
as Crito cried,
spied the ship from Delos
with its Delian sick and dying,
and turns to Socrates saying:
"I suggest you escape—
 use your get out of jail free card, cuz
the sour hermeneutic is in full sail,
Fate and friend *hypónoia*
have disembarked
bearing sickly-green bad news.

An Easter Summer Day

We caught the fish
and pulled it, big-thumbed
plum-from-pudding-from-water
thick and muddy that smelled
like dust and cow breath.
The broken tree its two great veins
of root bending to the water
there beneath where it was deep the bullhead
murky and clay-breathed
spat blind clouds of black pollywogs
to bob in chatty fat groups
at the shore's edge.
Theorizing how big the universe was,
we caught this big one
still cold with clay and fight,
the two-barbed hook vectored in the belly
which we pulled and brought to light
innards past to present—we were not sorry
but looked for the back-fin bone
which had poison my brother said,
and stood on end
like the hanged man's part
an alert and eager failure
big-eyed, bug-eyed, fish-eyed
blood on the grass
rising
to some water's surface.

On Easter
we threw him blood and guts back
to sink demon-faced into the clay hole
to return to the place we were
sure he would rise again; we always
returned the big ones this way.

Bonaparte in Austria

To glide again traceless
through casual slaughter
in the single wood,
the treachery of a warm Austrian sun
watching it all,
September no better, strewing bodies
like dust motes in an air so still
it stops the moment
and opens the place
where a sword cuts
into French-blue wool
with delivery and message,
channeling startled ichor
into small puddles.

He pitches forward forgetting
how heroism pools
and dampens the Hapsburg soil,
his time-rooted body
looted, they sling him into a ditch
on top of piles of broken blue,
to the place of cover up
where two hundred years later
he wakes to ditchdiggers digging
for a sewer,
his Christian skull still clinging convert-like
to his helmet, his absent eyes staring
as the ditchdiggers lining the trench
look on and sip their coffee.

The rupture unearths clay and silt,
makes the *Soldat* die again
and the living pause long enough
to ruin the day with delay.

The Seventeen Year Cicada

This 17th anniversary the unspeakable red-eyed
insect claiming spring and madness, maenads wild
with yawning desire unspeakable disaffection buried
alive the lines of Fata Morgana
all leggy convection Persephone
drawing up her skirts kicking high this desolate region
alive with crawling desire, the leer and sleepy grapple
of tiny claws that grasp what there is
to grasp—tree, arm, leaf, love.

The brittle corpses gather to argue the case
we seek the Other
we long to escape even to Hades, if need be
to the seasons of fallow to follow the Lonely Lord down
dragging his winter bride behind him, he means
no harm but knows no better.
She warms his dead soul's seasons
til her mom takes her back
and brings the elegant season to tingle with color.

Yet, she clings to the places
steepest and deepest and deadest
in the craggy ravines
where love dies quickly
and leaves behind the remains of many empty days,
the ex-o-skeletons of desire shed
by the graceless thousands,
as brown clumps of leaves fall
from the high reaches of love
and autumn disappears into the mouth of winter.

Flying on my 50th

Flying on my 50th
I glide above that gnostic petulance
that otherwise stalls me midair
and drops me down and back
toward fetal waters that lay like cenotes
and fill the places of deepest fear
with the sweet taste of eudaimonia.

Flying on my 50th
the lift of many-fingered love
under my wings raises me, yes
like Lazarus from a many tiered deadness,
the gift of feather and gravity arguing
me over the crossroads of despair
where rebel souls linger and suffer
for sidestepping Fate.

Flying on my 50th
reveals some things
I'd rather not see,
churns my stomach,
I vomit and wish
only for return . . .
The runway looms
and spreads itself wide
to seduce me downward
and guide me home,
this relationship looks like
another touch and go.

Reading Seamus Heaney

I move letter by letter through "the Spirit World"
across the goat-stained badly furled terrain
eaten by worms and desire
already in Qumran cave #4 ducking low
the sandstone rubbed raw with the scent
of countless religious animals
marking their territory,
he stands out scruffy.

Against the man-made cistern and shadow,
the scurvy proselytizer
bobs for converts like apples
in the sacred waters, every parsed catechumen
red-lipped and cool.

Nothing left in that poem
only the pious smell of psoriasis,
the cloister taste of day-old vision.

Fellow seers high atop poles
starving for some decent dying
breathe envy with their every breath,
from their anchorholds they squint to see

John the foul
bottling the waters of life
In cave #4.

For Jim was simple/And rain or shine he'd make his desperate rounds...
"Two Stick Drawings" Seamus Heaney

This Afternoon

In this afternoon
of poetic means and balmy winds,
the bond of disconnect loosens and trots us down
the paths of time echoic,
telling stories of saurian tragedy
implicating us in our existential shortness of breath.

In this afternoon the late summer leaves rustle,
silvery and wise and whisper
like Dodona's oaks in cypher—
every bit as oracular and commercial
it commands our attention,
answers the questions
if we will be happy
if our ship will come in
when will we die and how
this provides gainful employment
for poets and charlatans.

The decline is on, more or less,
says the majority of leaves,
first, a crinkle then a wheezing in the stoma
terminal with creaky valves, breathing slows
exhales the thought we have to do it over
and get it right, *samsara* waiting in the wings of autumn.

We droop half-heartedly knowing that,
tire with Angst and are ready
to give ourselves over
to morphing
to indemnifying the stolen green of our lives
with the hidden colors of wisdom,
while confessing arcane confidences that can't be shared.

Like the tethered dog
who forgets and runs
the full length of his chain,
looking to bite or maul
and gets snapped back with a yelp
and an instructive flop in the dirt,
we run the length of our days
at full speed until *O snap* there we lay
cartoonish and curled in a whirl of dust,
only to stare and become religious
at the limits of our love.

Ornamental Plant

Let's add an ornamental plant
to our house
our lives a tru green choice
that will bring
years of color to our fading happiness.
A plant that is true, faithful, willing
to live and die
and live again with the seasons
we watch with so much trepidation.

And if your plant comes balled and burlapped
as some are
make sure
to free the roots
(A made for TV drama)
And unshroud the burlap
(a made for church sermon).

Choose a plant
that is not pest-prone
that is seasonally brave
that remembers for you
these rhythms that gyre
the color chart will tell you

Rhododendrons do well but
azaleas need sun
and impatiens the best
They will live
Forever.

The Birth of Achilles

No foamy wave bearing love
could quicken the life to be,
only mischief to measure the slight—
Disinvited from the freakish fete,
she pleasures herself with mock hurt
and vows to ruin the ruttish affair—
this mortal sniffing the backside of
his fish goddess.

She sparks a war with envy,
slipstreams her way among the hoi polio.
All dressed up and denied an invite,
the second-tier goddess tosses
her apple and watches them scramble
this thing of joy and death.
Peleus, beige-brown and sanguine
Thetis, sea-green and nymphic
nod and smile as the Olympians do
they enjoy the mortal day and wave to Apollo
as he descends into the sea.

The winds of Ilion rush down back canyons
from that dark future
whistling through this horsehair cavalcade
of Corinthian misery
peddling furiously, drafting this tired poem
bucking the wind comically,
the echelon of riders lost in lactic acid
pant group-wise—a large clot
moving to a place of blockage and pileup
like dirty foam on a black beach
blown by Aegean winds
we flutter and look for that just-spawned goddess.

Hegel

It's such a short time
to read Hegel he writes
as if having taken
apart a Mercedes and having
put it back together laughs,
this jester of sobriety and complete sentences.
Every word ground smooth and buffed shiny
fits the improvidence precisely,
fits the diagram in 3-D inside his head
the spidery tendrils that reprimand
his heart without regard
for green defiles, and white cliffs, for the slung peaks
pulling us diminishing us dispersing us
in the backstreets of that high idealism
that fails to connect us,
lets go our hand and loses us
forever in the backstreets of Otherness.

I confuse Hegel with Kant
but there is no confusion it seems
he is he—both ontological liquidators
their buyouts stacked to the ceiling
all junk they sell late in the evening
at prices out of this world.

This morning my oatmeal tastes
like that, if ideas could have a taste,
like diesel and cilantro mixed
with butter and brine—criminal

I release it on its own recognizance
certainly not mine,
my criminal smallness sublated
by a Transcendental Ego
with a fun and roomy feel.

First Phobia

I am afraid I will write a book
thinking it will take someone's life
before I finish or
because I finish or
regardless if I finish—

This logic reigns supreme, yet
I give no credence to that tepid weather
that drives us so unpredictable,
our comings and goings, phenomena
we search for clues of who we might be.

Science tells us sells us
vaccines that do what they say they do
mostly, a novel approach to the fear of self
I yell nonetheless:
"False gods," in the face of science, which stares me down
"Sheesh," I say, "Ok."
The reprise instructive like the prophets of old
trying out their very first predictions
in small and stammering voices:
"The end is coming. You best be good!"

So, or yet, I am sure
I am killing something with all this
that waits to dance me into the catafalque
on a moonlit night of do-goodery,
so nearly day I can't tell, I shudder.
The menhirs of longing standing in a bendy row,
shifting their weight from side to side
like acned boys at a high school dance
pudgy with cryptic imperatives

that send hormones streaming
everywhere in excess.

The first dance on the plains of Stonehenge,
the first promises whispered
and gestations felt no different than now,
or in the caves of Malta
time alone, patriarchal and assuming,
they chant to that Moloch god
smacking his lips like Cronos to come.

It rises up like field stones
these things beneath us in us
squeezed by design flaws
that force it up—we stand accused
of crimes that claim no innocence
of trepidation that claims no cure.
We mark the deep cave's wall
with handprints by way of speaking.
We mark the darkness
with wishes by way of believing.

Kiwis from Chile!

…talking about odd, kiwis
from Chile make no sense—
this place-bound fruit
wishing to live elsewhere,
goes to great lengths and widths
to have its bio-urgent way
and propagate
like Greek colonists in open rebellion
with their metro-polis mom
or kon tiki raftsmen drifting east following the sun
and the possibility of new germination
sneaking away from extinction
like feral teenagers avoiding boredom.

"This kiwi is tart and sweet, all the way from Chile—
an odd place for kiwis to grow," I throw out,
"genetically modified, no doubt but tart
like Montmorency cherries."

Some conversation is better left phatic—
slurping ice cream atop a sugar cone I state
Hmm tasty, tart—no need to say more,
and am semantic millimeters away from speaking
in terms of appropriation and centering the conversation
of my uninteresting wants and needs
on the dogma of Otherness
that refutes me and them!

Not able or interested in distinguishing between those two,
I add silence to stew the unspoken legitimacy
and irrefutable argument—half truths far tastier than whole lies—

an acquired taste, the politicians will tell you.
This flavor prompts me to declare:

"I enjoy a good kiwi, my diet allows me one or two…"
but I cannot imagine how this simple thought
becomes a religion
that offers neither hope nor afterlife
only redemption which seems
little more than a poor meal
of processed fat and fatuity in caloric excess.

Exercising my mouth parts, anticipating kiwi succulence
I think, it is important
that everyone knows I like a good kiwi
not only for what it is,
but also for what it can become
which reminds me of my potential…

I enjoy a good kiwi with a degree of profundity
and historical sense that sweetens and tartens
this hour of matins
in this late and sun-bent afternoon,
we share agreeable enthusiasms
and see funny faces form among dust motes.

I gush with amazement
that Aldis sells kiwis from Chile,
this world a TV necromancer
that entertains with evolution
but dissolves at last in smoke rings
of lazy conscience and lingering indifferences.

In the world of everyday talk
kiwis need no introduction or exegesis
yet we insist they mean more
and offer raison d'etres that oppose
the snitty and commonplace ignorance
that passes for simple virtue or honesty
or populist religion stunned and snaky
with craziness . . .

So how do you think they came here? Kiwis I mean
by plane? I see them
buckled up all in a row fuzzy and anxious
trying to get their tray tables down or up
with a kind of happy difficulty
that fails to recognize the lack of hands,
the moment recedes as a memory of
childhood with some love in the mix—
stiff and stupid and funny, foolish:

We will always have the kiwis from Chile.

The Panopticon

That cross-eyed look of love
sees all and everywhere
watches you pace your cell,
hears the echoes of your crime reverberate.
From the panopticon of my heart,
I study your criminal emotion
as would a scientist
with charts and numbers, theories and thoughts,
and dissect that swollen sin
to learn your secret langue,
to watch you raise your eyes
as if raising a *Blutfahne* mumbling
"I take no prisoners," as you recall long lines
of droopy heads moving forward slowly
to the scimitar blunted by so many
loppings—the dust and diffidence
keeping sentinel to it all.

My single eye sees all, sometimes and always;
it attaches sensors to your head you feel but can't see,
your eyes sunk in grief and stupefaction,
Thanatos and *Eros* diffracted
through a prism of pity and grief
that diffuses light and dark.
I watch you fidget like a school child
waiting for recess.

Like Bentham, I will keep you honest,
terrorize you with that omniscience—
the single watchman who plays roulette with longing—
until that day
I release you
from the panopticon of my heart
that has watched you forever.

Icarus

It wasn't that far a fall
feather and all
from the aerie reaches
of heaven's backside,
as if shot for sport
by a burly and bored Cupid
hitting the mark every other time
the hallow bone,
whistling that love
is nothing more than winged flesh falling.

He watches
it ride the wind at the stern of the storied liner—
this prescience iridescent with memory
"Pull, shoot," someone says
the cloying clay disappears in a poof of dust
over churlish waters pestered
by gulls swooping for garbage.

On his less than sturdy angel-things
the wings that
glide him upward
at the wrong angle of intent,
he feels love grow sullen and waxy
heavy with hubris;

it brings the contraption
to heel
to ruin
to ground
to naught.

Icarus falls through the shallow air
to the whistle of hollow wing-bone
and rustle of feather in denial,
the wings of passion
unable to support
the weight of love.

He tumbles back to earth
on the less than sturdy angel things
thinking someday
I will learn to fly.

Rich Folks Beggar

the question why they should care
they wear their arrhythmic hearts thin
on foreshortened sleeves,
those polo shirts two sizes too small to hide its throbbing.

Hunched and hurried, they breech birth
their thoughts on the matter, you can only imagine
the difficulty they stare *agape* in the face thinking
"how homely this love!"

Their legs languish, their spirits blue and suffocated
they carry to term nonetheless
the feeble other, a successor yawny and unfit
for a world so wide of virtue
so short on grace;
it arrives with a face
rumpled and rippled by that G force that pulls and yanks,
smushes and wobbles the physiognomic purchase
that makes them homeless, squats them squarely
in front of their own large places.
They note the garbage everywhere,
their broken childhood loves nowhere
to be found.

They wish to be Charlton Heston
and commandeer a Red or Sargasso Sea
commanding it to open and part for them
or like Canute on a beach as frothy as the waves he tells to stop,
they don't, of course, nothing halts
their ponderous words and derogated privilege
that cracks and fissures like patio pavers

broken and aged in circular tumble bins
that leaves them looking old and wizened,
porous to the delusions of antique significance.

Their first words of supplication
happen cloudy and pointless,
the predilection for dressing them up
in religious thought, swaddling nakedness
in the droopy, ratty and torn cloth of bad faith
they lay there on the sidewalk in garbage
that looks like everyone else's.

Speaking ignorance to truth
the cadences of polite religiosity
lull and liquify that civil kindness that
remains stuck in the craw of good intention
until the gag reflex—time and its disavowal,
betrayal and its bickering—spill the wastrel contents
onto sidewalks and stoops of the haggard Brownstones,
the second coming of the garbage trucks some ways off.

Fibonacci Dance

I stand in line nervous,
shifting my weight
from leg to leg
favoring immortality
with unreflected upon humility,
hoping in big and droopy words to be saved,
I guess, to learn the *Danse* Steps *Macabre*
using the Arthur Murray method—
jerking this way and that,
planting a foot here and there.
I step on her toes; she smiles and says
"It is so much like life!" this late and glib philosophy
disrupts my concentration.

I wish I could dance
this *danse* with upright grace
and solemn dignity yet
revel like a thieving kobold
in the ancient patterns of inscribed beauty.

To put it mathematically, I wish
I were a Fibonacci sequence—
a shell, a tree, a flower—
with my own agile arrangements of beauty
confirming the sacred speech of the universe.

I wish I could dance the *danse* with even temperament
and glide over that eternity-pocked ballroom floor
with aplomb and generosity and if that wish
does not come true
then teach me the jitterbug
and it will do.

The Kyrie and Higgs Boson Anxiety

Autumn winds pinch, the leaves rise
in windrows tumbled about by vortices
funneling faith into crazy curls
and bookish ciphers
that taunt the winter with thoughts
of spring and resurrection.

It slams its fists, in the face of day
this Irish masher, stupid
blows that sting and stun this grey slate day.
With veins blue and bubbling
a voice bent and scratchy
the Kyrie Eleison rises as incense rises
begging for simple favors—the kind
that rocks in a chair on a dirty porch
and spits chaw into a coke bottle.

The elusive boson pays no attention—
let them beg for mercy,
make Him talk that way if you wish
gibberish to us, his broken children
who prefer secrecy and smallness,
math and machines.

This autumn gathers itself up,
pulling at its pants unable to top the belly
of winter to come, the god-boson
iridescent and infinitesimal, crisp as an apple
jubilant as light, opting for fame elsewhere.

The morning strains acapella,
Sunday angling toward collision,
the science of faith and fear
the very small and violent, look to winter
for respite and requiem.

An Early Morning Satellite

moves in an early morning sky
against the night
pretending to be
a star that forgets once dead,
to die it sends its light instead as if
a taunt
that streaks across the darkish dawn
with an intelligence chased by a scruffy pack
of dog-faced blackness
sniffing the brevity of light
waiting for it to falter
to fall on a single knee, they circle and close
neither angry nor vengeful
merely grey then black.

But for the time
Being it shines brightly and obeys the rules
of impersonation, fleeing
like clockwork right to left
etching a diamond rut along the blue horizon
that delivers caesarean a time abated light
nipped at howled at feeding
the darkness.

We wish upon that pretend star, twinkle and all,
and enjoin that currish darkness never
to overtake the immovable sky.

Morning Train (the Book of Genesis)

The train slinks
under callused hands in an autumnal night,
petted and stroked and loved for being other and absent;
it collapses its spine to that needy touch,
purrs expectant with entitled diffidence
as if Love were its due
and careless Affection its right.

It arches its back contrapuntally
and in early evening in serene ardor
scatters its siren sound to an empty universe announcing
the ebb and flow of distance and space
time and eternity as Doppler humor.

About the Author

Steven Joyce is an Associate Professor of German and comparative studies at the Ohio State University, Mansfield campus. He is the recipient of several Fulbright awards and has published a book on G. B. Shaw entitled *Transformations and Texts* as well as a number of poems in literary journals including *Kimera* and *Red River Review* and *Minimus*. His award-winning book of essays entitled *The Winds of Ilion* appeared in 2011 and a book of poetry, *The Apostate Djin,* an Indie Book Award finalist, appeared in 2013. He holds a Ph. D. in comparative literature from UNC-Chapel Hill and has published a number of articles on literary theory and criticism.